MASTERING THE ART
OF
SELF-EXPRESSION

A Creative Journaling Workbook

Laura Thoma

Karen,

Happy Journaling!

Laura Thoma

SassyQuackProDucktions, LLC
Guilford, CT

Dedicated to my younger self, who never stopped believing in the power of creating, and to all who feel lost and are searching for themselves.

ISBN: 978-1-365-66965-1

Personal Growth/Creativity
All photography © Laura Thoma

SassyQuackProDucktions, LLC
4 Hickory Road
Guilford, CT 06437

Acknowledgements

ACKNOWLEDGEMENTS

I am beyond grateful for the support, opinions, and the occasional kick in the pants from my wife, Chris Wolak, and friends Cyndy Ciolino and Chris Acton.

A heartfelt thank you to Kevin Sandstrom of Blick Art Materials in Wheaton, IL. Without his early belief and support in my work Mastering the Art of Self-Expression would not exist.

Much gratitude to all the women who have gathered in my various Creative Journaling Groups and Workshops over the years. You have encouraged me to capture what we do in person and share it with others so that they may explore the power of Creative Journaling in a variety of ways online. Through your playfulness and insights you have also inspired me to continue to create new recipes and adventures for all of us.

I would like to give a special thank you to those women who contributed their creative play for this workbook: Chris Acton, Cyndy Ciolino, Margaret Doyle, Kathy Knapp, and Barb Marden. You are inspiring others to reclaim their refrigerator art!

As you all did, I know others will...

Come for the Crayons, Stay for the Connections!℠

Your journal is a place to...

Explore

Discover

Play

Once you make a decision, the universe conspires to make it happen. — Ralph Waldo Emerson

Table of Contents

To thine
own self
be true...
--William
Shakespeare

doodle, ponder, brainstorm...

Introduction

Welcome to **Mastering the Art of Self-Expression.** Creative Journaling is a form of visual journaling that reconnects you to yourself. You'll find yourself in the pages of your journal by exploring the power of play, reclaiming your refrigerator art, and practicing consistent self-expression.

I developed Creative Journaling as I was ending my first career as a professional dancer. I was feeling lost and unsure of my creative abilities outside the world of dance. I turned to the creative activities I had loved as a child: cutting, pasting, coloring, and journaling. I allowed myself the freedom to play and explore with no rules. I started pasting all the pictures that caught my eye and allowed myself to doodle and draw without judgment. Slowly I began to rediscover myself in the pages of my journal. It was an amazing reunion with my creative spirit.

As I began to share my experience with others, I realized how many people had "outgrown" their creative side, which inspired me to create the first Creative Journaling 101 Workshop. There was so much enthusiasm for the work and requests to meet again that I formed a monthly group. Each month I created new exercises for us to explore. As we played together, I realized the need to name and create templates for the exercises.

After seeing the movie Julie and Julia it hit me—what I had created were recipes. Recipes that each individual could try, as is, then experiment with and tweak for their own taste. I had forgotten how inspired I had been as a kid watching Julia Child's cooking show on PBS. She always made cooking and creating look so fun and possible. She was fearless with no worries. If you messed up, it was just "you alone in the kitchen." I will always remember her cake with the caramelized dome top made on a metal mixing bowl. When the dome had set, she placed it above a chocolate cake and shattered it — forever becoming my hero. How had I forgotten Julia? It was amazing to rediscover her as an adult. I was truly inspired by her life story—that she had accomplished at a mature age what many might have felt she'd been too old to even begin. As I began my second career, Julia reminded me that it was never too late and that I was never too old to find a new passion and calling.

In honor of Julia I have designed this recipe book after her first cookbook, Mastering the Art of French Cooking. This workbook is meant to get dirty, so carry it with you, doodle on it, and don't worry about spills. Make it your own—write in the margins, tweak the recipes to your liking, get it messy and have fun Mastering The Art of Self-Expression!

Creatively yours,
Laura

PLAYTIME
IS
IMPORTANT

make a date
with you

doodle, ponder, brainstorm...

Creativity Snacks

I was introduced to the magic of daily practice in the world of dance. I found my daily practice at the ballet barre to be a nurturing experience that taught me three very important lessons. One, consistency is the key to growth. Two, consistency breeds motivation, confidence, and eventual mastery. And three, investing time in yourself and your passion will enhance your life in ways you can scarcely imagine.

On our journey through Creative Journaling, the first stop is the Creativity Snack. A Creativity Snack is a tool used to practice daily consistency. This tool will teach you many things: the power of self-expression, creating for creation's sake, time management, self observation, releasing all-or-nothing thinking, interrupting perfectionism, and developing curiosity, to name a few.

In this workbook I feature several sizes of Creativity Snacks that will vary in time and complexity, so you will have a variety to choose from. Just like your body needs food for fuel, so does your creative spirit need play for power. In many ways Creativity Snacks are a form of meditation or a practice in centering yourself. You will learn through this practice to listen to yourself, to access your creativity when you want it or need it, and to release your drive for right and wrong. You will begin to recognize your own excuses and to embrace and express your thoughts, emotions, and opinions while strengthening your creative muscles.

All you need is this recipe book, a blank journal, a kitchen timer, and a few other items you'll gather together in one place (see page 9). The guidelines are simple: set your timer for the allotted time and when the timer goes off, you're done. That's right, you're done. Now, for all my perfectionists, I know how hard this is—after all, I am a recovering perfectionist myself. But the idea is that we learn to break mental patterns. "I don't have the right supplies." "If things aren't perfect, I'm not going to do them." Or the ever famous —"If there's not enough time to finish, I'm not going to start!" Sound familiar?

So start small. Begin with appetizers and work up to entrees. In the beginning the time constraints may cause some anxiety and even frustration—but keep with it and trust the process. Soon you will have forged a true partnership with your creative side and will have reclaimed the power of play. You will enjoy exploring yourself and the world around you with a newfound freedom of self-expression.

Let's get started!

doodle, ponder, brainstorm...

Reclaim Your Refrigerator Art

Remember when you used to bring home your drawings and paintings and proudly display them on the fridge? Well, it's time to reclaim that zest for creativity.

Don't worry if you're someone who didn't have anyone who supported or nurtured your creative side. You do now! All of us have a natural creative spirit that many of us lose along the way. Some of us are taught to outgrow it and some of us are told we don't have "talent." But we are here to celebrate life— the way we see it and experience it, through our own eyes.

So I'm going to ask you to write a permission slip to play on the first page of your journal. Permission to allow yourself to doodle and color and create whatever you want without judgment. Give yourself the permission and encouragement you need to make your journal a safe space to reclaim your refrigerator art!

Remember to sign and date it!

Release Your Inner Artist

your life is
your canvas

doodle, ponder, brainstorm...

Appetizers

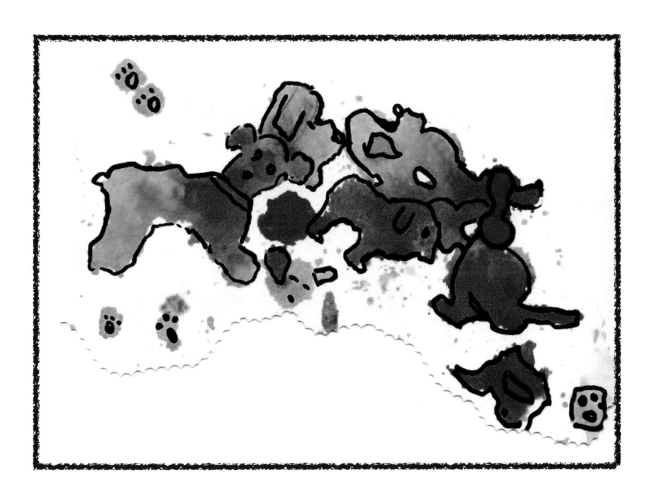

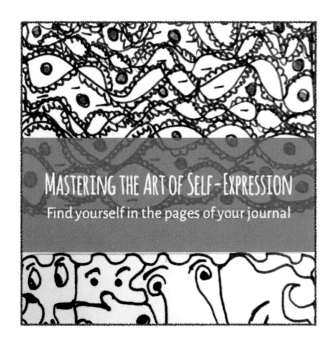

MASTERING THE ART OF SELF-EXPRESSION

Find yourself in the pages of your journal

doodle, ponder, brainstorm...

Appetizer Introduction

An **Appetizer** is meant to get your creative juices flowing. It's a taste, a warm-up. It'll give you a chance to practice using your Creativity Snacks and address the "I don't have time" excuse because it never takes more than 15 minutes.

Using a recipe: I suggest that you read each recipe through at least once before you start. Try each recipe the first time "as is." Afterwards, use the corresponding note page to jot down what you liked, what challenged you, and what you might want to tweak next time you try the recipe. I encourage you to sign and date your work for two reasons. One, to help you own it. And two, to allow you to see your growth and change over time.

Reserve a creative space: Find a place where you'll be able to create without having to clean up before you begin. That becomes one of our greatest excuses not to create: we spend our time "straightening things up" instead of creating something. So pick a chair and stash a tv tray near it that you can pull out. Or find a corner where you can put up a card table. Once you have your space claimed, you'll need some supplies.

The supplies you'll need are: A blank journal—make sure it's big enough that you won't feel cramped when you're working in it. Choose a container to create what I call a **Snack Pack** in which to keep your supplies or "ingredients." Collect markers or colored pencils or crayons or all of the above if you wish. You'll also need scissors and different types of fasteners such as glue, tape, or staples. Gather some different types of paper with varying colors and patterns. Old wrapping paper, greeting cards, and pamphlets from museums or rest stops are fun to have on hand as well as a small assortment of magazines. Lastly, gather together what I like to call **spices**, random bits and pieces like stickers, gems, stamps, ribbon, anything that you like the texture and color of will be great (these are referred to in the recipes as spices). Remember, there is no right or wrong. The goal is to have supplies on hand, so you don't waste time wandering around looking for what you want or need.

Presentation helps engage your creative side: Many of us are visual, so think about what you like to look at. Would it excite you to see all your markers in a clear glass? Or would you rather have a beautiful old box that holds all of your creative elements? Whichever it is, create storage that gets you and keeps you excited about your creative explorations.

Use what you've gathered: Practice using what you have. Add to it as you find fun new things. Practice using what you've gathered—interrupt the mental pattern that needs the "perfect" element. Don't have what you're looking for? Try something else!

What I like about this recipe is...

Thoughts and insights...

Tweaks to try next time...

Description: Zine Grab is all about diving in and not overthinking. It also allows you to think about yourself in different ways. It's a great way to practice the power of play.

Ingredients:
Journal
Magazine or torn out pictures
Glue or paste
Markers
Scissors
"Spices," any you like
Kitchen timer

Directions:
1. Choose a time frame (5–15 minutes) and set your timer.
2. Randomly grab a picture from your stack or tear one out (don't overthink).
3. Next ask yourself, "How does this picture represent me?"
4. Write about how the picture is like you. Maybe it reminds you of a specific event in your life. Does it bring to mind a goal or dream, or maybe a personality trait? You can add anything you want to the page — have fun with it!
5. When the timer goes off, you're done. Sign and date your page.

Hints & Options:
1. Don't overthink this exercise, it is a warm-up just to get you going.
2. You could also ask yourself how your picture is different from you.
3. Sometimes wearing a funky artist hat makes this exercise more fun, less serious, and therefore more successful.

Recipe: Zine Grab

What I like about this recipe is...

Thoughts and insights...

Tweaks to try next time...

Description: **Zine Grab 2** is all about words. You want to practice reacting to your instincts. You'll be amazed at how the words speak to you when you put them together.

Ingredients:
Journal
Magazine, catalog, or newspaper
Glue, tape, or stapler
Markers
Scissors
"Spices," any you like
Kitchen timer

Directions:
1. Choose a time frame (5–15 minutes), but set your timer for half of your time. For example, if you plan to spend 15 minutes, set the timer for 7.
2. Pick a magazine. Flip through and cut or tear out any words that speak to you.
3. When your timer goes off stop tearing things out.
4. Reset your timer for the remaining half of your time and start adhering words to your page.
5. When the timer goes off, you're done.
6. Ponder what your finished page says to you.
7. Jot down important insights.
8. Sign and date your page.

Hints & Options:
1. Don't overthink this exercise. It is a warm-up just to get you going.
2. Play with putting the words in different patterns or directions.
3. Sometimes drinking a beverage from a curly straw makes this exercise more fun, less serious, and therefore more successful.

Recipe: Zine Grab 2

What I like about this recipe is...

Thoughts and insights...

Tweaks to try next time...

Description: Spice Trio pays homage to all the design, art, and cooking shows that give participants different elements to put together to create a cohesive piece.

Ingredients:
Journal
Random spices
Think of a theme, Ex. daydreaming
Glue or paste
Markers
Scissors
Kitchen timer

Directions:
1. Choose a time frame (5–15 minutes) and set your timer.
2. Randomly pick 3 spices.
3. Write your theme on your page.
4. Create a page based on this theme using your 3 random spices.
5. When the timer goes off, you're done. Sign and date your page.

Hints & Options:
1. Create a mixture of random spices, think of it as a spice rub, and store them in their own container. Only have one of something left? Toss it in your spice rub. This way you always have a unique assortment to embellish and flavor your recipes.
2. Start a theme bag or box. Every time you find a theme or quote that speaks to you, write or type it out and put it in your box. Remember, nothing is off limits. Nothing is too broad or too focused.
3. With this appetizer, try not to plan. Just take your spices and see where they lead—you might be surprised!

Recipe: Spice Trio

What I like about this recipe is...

Thoughts and insights...

Tweaks to try next time...

Description: Inky-Dinky brings out the kid in you while you learn about color mixing and design. This Snack can be done in one or two sessions.

Ingredients:
Journal
Watercolor paper (optional)
Straw
Food coloring
Sharpies: black and bold colors
Newspaper
Plastic garbage bag
Scissors
Kitchen timer

Directions:
1. Set your timer for 15 minutes.
2. Cover work surface with the garbage bag then cover with newspaper for absorption.
3. Pick 2 or 3 colors of food coloring.
4. Tear a page from your journal or use watercolor paper.
5. Drip several drops of each food color onto your paper.
6. Take your straw and blow the food coloring around. Rotate paper.
7. Let it dry.
8. Set your timer again and see what you see in your Inky-Dinky.
9. Use your Sharpies to make it come alive.

Hints & Options:
1. Do the Snack on two consecutive days to allow for drying time.
2. Play with your color—stand over paper, get down beneath it, try different amounts of force when blowing through the straw.
3. Remember to leave your journal open so your page can dry completely.
4. For inspiration, try wearing tie-dye while you're enjoying this Snack.

Recipe: Inky-Dinky

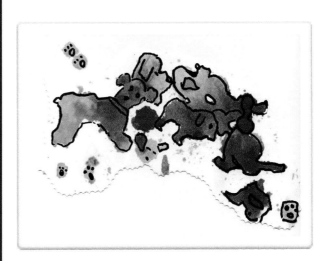

What I like about this recipe is...

Thoughts and insights...

Tweaks to try next time...

Description: 2 Paper Tango is a great way to learn to play with contrast.

Ingredients:
Journal
1 or 2 pieces of solid colored paper
1 or 2 pieces of patterned paper
Sharpies/markers: black and bold colors
Scissors (plain or fancy patterned)
Glue or paste
Kitchen Timer

Directions:
1. Choose a time frame (5–15 minutes) and set your timer.
2. Choose a piece of paper to be the lead, a strong base piece.
3. Cut that piece into any shape you like.
4. Next, choose the piece of paper that will be the follow, the accent.
5. Plan and design how to accent your original shape.
6. Play with the positioning of the papers to discover their dance.
7. Glue the pieces together and attach them to your journal.
8. Use your markers to embellish your design if you'd like.
9. When the timer goes off, you're done. Sign and date your page.

Hints/Options:
1. Use two pieces of colored paper and make patterns with your markers.
2. Remember, there is no right or wrong!
3. Make several small dances and glue them on the same page in your journal. What story do they tell?
4. Wear a rose in your hair or hold it in your teeth to get you in the mood.

Recipe: 2 Paper Tango

What I like about this recipe is...

Thoughts and insights...

Tweaks to try next time...

Description: Squiggle Turn encourages you to see things from different perspectives. It's always fun and often surprising.

Ingredients:
Journal
One bright Sharpie
Crayons, pastels, colored pencils, markers or all of the above!
Kitchen timer

Directions:
1. Choose a time frame (5–15 minutes) and set your timer.
2. Commence to Squiggle Turn!
3. Take your bold Sharpie and make a random squiggle on the page.
4. Next, spin your journal with both hands.
5. Stop it by placing your finger straight down.
6. What do you see? What does your squiggle look like from this angle?
7. Grab your other crayons and pencils and flesh out what you see!
8. When the timer goes off, you're done. Sign and date your page.

Hints & Options:
1. Turn your journal slowly instead of spinning it and see what is revealed.
2. After you squiggle try closing your journal and then reopen and see what you find.
3. Don't overthink! Just go with your first instinct and let the form lead you.
4. Stand up and walk around the table until you see something in your squiggle.
5. Try nibbling on a licorice whip for inspiration.

Recipe: Squiggle Turn

What I like about this recipe is...

Thoughts and insights...

Tweaks to try next time...

Description: Letter & Number comes from my days of watching <u>Sesame Street</u>. You're going to feature a number and a letter. So today this snack is brought to you by the letter __ and by the number __. Have fun!

Ingredients:
Journal
Magazine
Paper: patterned or blank
Crayons, markers, or colored pencils
Glue
Dice (optional)
Scissors
Kitchen timer

Directions:
1. Choose a time frame (5-15 minutes) and set your timer.
2. Pick a number and a letter (or let a roll of the dice choose for you).
3. Create a page using the letter and the number you choose.
4. When the timer goes off, you're done. Sign and date your page.

Hints & Options:
1. Set your timer for 1 minute. Jump up and down, count your jumps until the timer goes off. This is your number. Reset your timer for 1 minute. Recite the alphabet continuously until the timer stops. This is your letter.
2. Play with creating patterns with your number or letter or both.
3. How many rings are you wearing? That's your number. The first letter of your childhood friend's last name is your letter.
4. For extra inspiration wear a Muppet T-shirt!

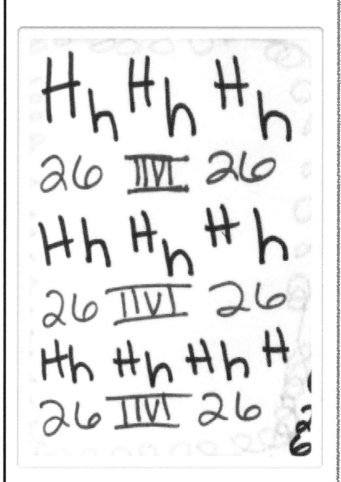

You can discover more about a person in an hour of play than in a year of conversation.

--Plato

doodle, ponder, brainstorm...

thomaOm

Explore your layers

doodle, ponder, brainstorm...

Entrée Introduction

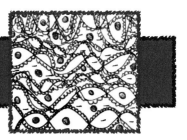

An **Entrée** is a heartier recipe that takes more time. This is a great place to start exploring your layers, how you think, and how you like to break things down. Remember, there is no right or wrong. Encourage yourself to try every recipe once.

Using a recipe: As with the appetizers, I suggest that you read the recipe through at least once before you start. Try each recipe the first time "as is." Afterwards, take notes about what you liked, what challenged you, and what you might want to add to the recipe next time.

Claiming a creative space: Now that you've had a creative space for a while you've seen the benefits. It's time to start scoping out where you can make a permanent creative space for yourself. It doesn't need to be large, in fact, a small closet is great and can be very self contained, with a built in work surface and shelves for spices. See if you can find an alcove or other unused space. Get creative.

Upgrade your supplies: As you work with markers and pencils you'll start to see what you like and what you don't. You don't have to spend a lot of money on supplies, but you will find that upgrading markers and colored pencils and such can make a big difference. Try taking yourself on a playdate to an art supply store and test out different brands. See what you like.

Presentation helps engage your creative side: After working with your journal and spices you probably have a better idea of what you like and what you find visually appealing. You don't have to spend a lot of money on organizing—get creative and find containers that speak to you. One of my favorite places to look for things is in junk shops. I love finding a unique container that beckons me to my supplies.

Use what you've gathered: Now that you have a better feel for your supplies get rid of what's not working. Donate them to your local library, school, or Girl Scout troop and refresh your stash. Once you've rejuvenated your spices again practice using what you have—interrupt the mental pattern that needs the "perfect" element. Don't have what you're looking for? Try something else! And remember to rotate your supplies every couple of months.

What I like about this recipe is...

Thoughts and insights...

Tweaks to try next time...

Description: Medadoodle is a form of moving meditation. The focus of the exercise is to teach yourself to get lost in the movement of doodling. We also use color as a catalyst to stay inspired in the moment. This is a great centering exercise that allows you to still your mind and be in the present moment.

Ingredients:
Journal
Markers or colored pencils
Kitchen timer

Directions:
1. Gather markers and/or pencils in colors that speak to your current mood.
2. Choose a time frame (30–45 minutes) and set your timer.
3. Start doodling. Try not to think—just get lost in the movement and color.
4. When your timer goes off, you're done. Sign and date your page.

Hints & Options:
1. The only "goal" when creating a Medadoodle is not to over-think. This is not about drawing, planning, or designing. It is about movement and being present to flow and color.
2. Choose only 3 colors in the same color palette and make a monochromatic Medadoodle.
3. Use only a black felt tip or ball point pen and create a Medadoodle in black and white.
4. Pick a theme and write it at the top of the page (example: New Job), then let yourself respond.
5. Put on music that inspires you and get lost in the music and movement.
6. Graham crackers and juice might be nice when your timer goes off!

Recipe: Medadoodle

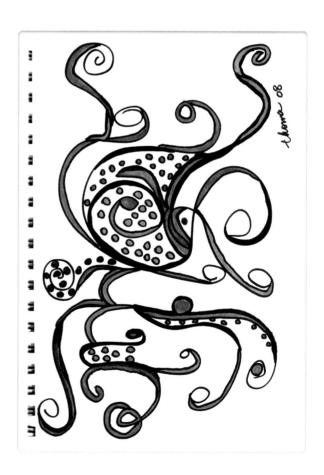

What I like about this recipe is...

Thoughts and insights...

Tweaks to try next time...

Description: **Dream Drop** is a visioning exercise which reminds you that, just like a drop of water creates a ripple of change, so can your vision.

Ingredients:
Journal, colored paper, magazines
Dream Drop template if desired (pg 53)
Glue and scissors
Markers, paint, colored pencils
2 timers

Directions:
1. Choose a time frame (30–90 minutes) and set your 1st timer.
2. Next pick a dream, something you want to create in your life: a hobby, a job you want, your life in 5 years.
3. Now close your eyes and imagine what the best version of your dream would be—what does it look like?
4. Choose 3–5 magazines and set your 2nd timer for 10–15 minutes.
5. Go hunting for images and words, remember not to over-think. Let the images talk to you. Just tear out what you like and put them aside.
6. When the timer goes off, you'll start to create your Dream Drop. You can use the template on page 53 or a blank page in your journal.
7. Feel free to embellish your drop.
8. When timer goes off, sign and date your page.

Hints & Options:
1. Make sure all your images reflect your dream and what you want.
2. Make your Dream Drop visually appealing to you, so you will want to look at it every day and focus on what you want to create in your life.
3. Look at your Dream Drop daily!
4. Visionaries often wear fancy hats… why not give it a try!

Recipe: Dream Drop

What I like about this recipe is...

Thoughts and insights...

Tweaks to try next time...

Description: Picture This Postcard is a fun way to savor the memories of an experience. It gives you a unique format to record your thoughts and feelings.

Ingredients:
Journal
2 pieces of blank colored paper
Magazines
Markers, pencils, or paint
Glue and scissors
Kitchen timer

Directions:
1. Set your timer for 30–90 minutes.
2. Pick an event, trip, or experience you want to record.
3. Cut both paper pieces down to 4X6"
4. Now you have the front and the back of your Picture This Postcard.
5. On the front of your postcard: collage, draw, or paint what you want to remember from the event, trip, or experience.
6. On the back: use words. Write a list, a story, or short blurbs of what you did and how you enjoyed it.
7. There is no right or wrong, so just play and have fun.
8. Last but not least, make a stamp for your postcard.
9. When the timer goes off, you're done. Sign and date your work.

Hints & Options:
1. This is actually a great recipe to make when traveling. You can either make postcards and include things you are seeing or buy postcards and journal on the back—punch a hole in the corner and keep them on a ring.
2. You can do this to manifest an experience in your life. Where would you like to go? Bon Voyage!
3. Inspire yourself by having a snack from your desired destination!

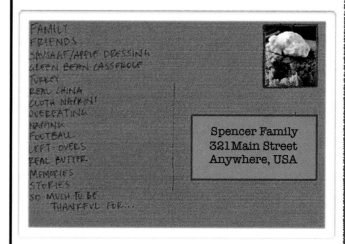

What I like about this recipe is...

Thoughts and insights...

Tweaks to try next time...

Description: **Textures & Patterns** is an exercise to get you thinking and creating in a different way. It's fun and challenging to create different designs.

Ingredients:
Journal
Funky paper or old greeting cards
Rubber stamps or colorful duct tape
Ribbon
Glue
Markers and pencils
Kitchen timer

Directions:
1. Choose a time frame (30–90 minutes) and set your timer.
2. Choose one element to start with: let's say, a stamp.
3. Start your pattern. A pattern can be many things: repetitive shape, sequence, or color combination.
4. Add in other spices as you desire.
5. Remember, there is no right or wrong. If you prefer to draw your pattern first then build up with texture, great. If you work better just following your instincts, fantastic! Let go and have fun!
6. When the timer goes off, stop where you are...I know it's tough! Sign and date your work.

Hints & Options:
1. If you are not a "pattern person," working in all one color or medium may suit you best when you start. It won't be as visually overwhelming.
2. Sometimes listening to music you really like will inspire you to create a rhythmic pattern.
3. Give yourself a theme like circles or triangles.
4. Give yourself a pattern such as: big, little, little, big, big.

Recipe: Textures & Patterns

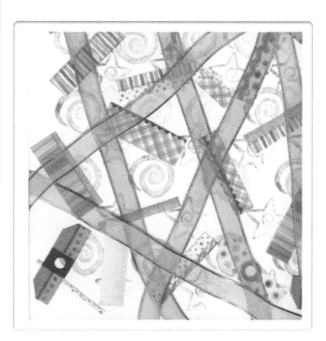

What I like about this recipe is...

Thoughts and insights...

Tweaks to try next time...

Description: Doodle Heads is a recipe designed to help you let go of "realistic" drawing and focus on faces and shapes.

Ingredients:
Journal
Markers or colored pencils
Magazine pictures or photographs
Kitchen timer

Directions:
1. Select several pictures of people whose faces speak to you.
2. Set your timer for 30 to 45 minutes.
3. Start with just the shape of the head.
4. Look at the features—what stands out to you?
5. Create a Doodle Head for each person you picked.
6. Create a background for your Doodle Heads. Are they on a quest? Are they traveling in Paris or perhaps just lounging in the garden?
7. When your timer goes off, you're done. Sign and date your page, shut your journal, and enjoy the rest of your day!

Hints & Options:
1. Allow yourself the freedom not to draw perfectly.
2. Using the Muppets or cartoon characters as models helps take the pressure off drawing.
3. Use your Doodle Heads to resolve feelings. Example: You've had a bad day at work. You had an argument with your boss. In the moment you didn't say what you wanted. Doodle Head you and your boss and write out what you wish you had said. Maybe draw your boss like the angry celery stick he resembles when he's upset. It's a great way to get your feelings out.

Recipe: Doodle Heads

What I like about this recipe is...

Thoughts and insights...

Tweaks to try next time...

Description: Mosaic Me is a recipe that reminds you of your own complexity. We often get defined by a single role and fall into the trap of believing it, which leaves us feeling one dimensional. Let's explore some other sides today.

Ingredients:
Journal
1 or 2 sheets of blank paper
Magazines or fun paper
Markers, scissors, glue
Kitchen timer

Directions:
1. Set your timer for 30–90 minutes.
2. Pick several areas of your life to focus on that don't usually get enough attention. For example: being a friend, an artist, a traveler, a cook, a gardener, etc.
3. Take your piece of paper and draw a shape on it—any shape you like.
4. Divide your shape into as many sections as you have areas of focus.
5. Assign each section a focus and label it—assign a number to the section so once you cut it out you can easily put it back together.
6. Cut out your pieces. Then write your focus and number on the back of each piece.
7. Next, decorate each section to represent its focus. You can be as literal or as abstract as you choose.
8. Once all the sections are complete, glue your mosaic into your journal and add descriptive words if you'd like.

Hints & Options:
1. Turn a tool belt into an artist belt to hold glue, markers, scissors, etc.
2. Stay curious, ask yourself questions about your mosaic, jot down notes.

Recipe: Mosaic Me

What I like about this recipe is...

Thoughts and insights...

Tweaks to try next time...

Description: **Inspired By** is an exciting recipe that really gets you motivated!

Ingredients:
Journal
Markers or colored pencils
Fun paper
A favorite quote
Kitchen timer

Directions:
1. Set your timer for 30–60 minutes.
2. Sit with your quote and read it over several times.
3. Ask yourself the following: What is it about this quote that speaks to me? How would I explain it to someone else? What would this quote look like visually?
4. Decide whether you want to write out your quote first and work from that or if you want to design your page and then include the quote at the end.
5. Remember, there is no right or wrong.
6. When the timer goes off, you're done. Sign and date your page.

Hints & Options:
1. Pick a quote that really speaks to you. Then respond to it visually.
2. Don't over-think. Let your instincts and intuition guide you.
3. Include in your own words what this quote means to you and why.
4. Designate a page in your journal to write quotes that speak to you. It's fun to write them in different color inks. You could also print them and glue them in.

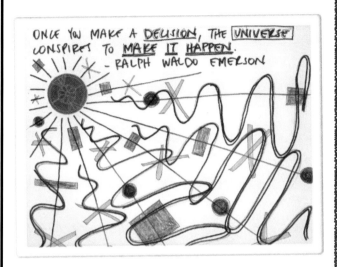

What I like about this recipe is...

Thoughts and insights...

Tweaks to try next time...

Description: **Word Art** is a powerful recipe that encourages you to explore the meanings of words that you've absorbed and made a part of your inner dialogue. It will teach you to reclaim and redefine these words for yourself.

Ingredients:
Journal
Markers or colored pencils
Kitchen timer

Directions:
1. Choose a time frame (30–90 minutes) and set your timer.
2. Think of a word that you struggle to accept: do you scoff when someone calls you beautiful? Do you struggle to call yourself successful?
3. Choose your word and write it the way it feels when you hear it. Play with color and font. Are the letters jagged or smooth? Tiny or huge?
4. Then write all the negative connotations of this word that come to mind. How would you describe it?
5. On a separate page write your word the way you'd like it to feel (see example).
6. Write words that would be connected to this new feeling—practice owning them.
7. When the timer goes off, you're done. Sign and date your pages.

Hints & Options:
1. If you struggle with being "negative" remember you are trying to flush this out and reclaim a word.
2. Words are very powerful. Allow yourself to reclaim those that have stifled you.
3. Don't edit yourself. Don't worry what anyone else would think. Just write the words that come to your mind. Sharing this exercise with a safe friend can be powerful and healing.

Recipe: Word Art

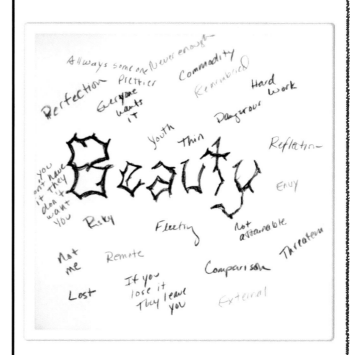

What I like about this recipe is...

Thoughts and insights...

Tweaks to try next time...

Description: Reflections in Black & White is a self-reflective recipe that will encourage insights around situations you feel trapped in.

Ingredients:
Journal
Number 2 pencil
Black pen (ink or marker)
Kitchen timer

Directions:
1. Set your timer for 30–45 minutes. (Entire exercise will take 60–90 minutes.)
2. Choose a challenging situation, a frustrating habit, a chronic pattern or an irritation.
3. Take a minute or two and write what it feels like to be trapped in the behavior, situation, or pattern.
4. Next, take your black pen and using shapes and lines express in black and white the feelings of the issue.
5. Take your time. Try to express what your situation looks and feels like.
6. When your timer goes off, set it again for 30–45 minutes.
7. Now grab your number two pencil and see if you can find the gray.
8. Don't over-think, just trust your instincts.
9. When the timer goes off, you're done. Sign and date your page.

Hints & Options:
1. This recipe works best when you can stay in touch with your feelings of being trapped. Don't be afraid to express how that feels.
2. When you're done with the recipe, take a moment to reflect — What has your drawing shown you? Has anything about the situation or pattern shifted? What has the gray shown you? Do you have any insights?

What I like about this recipe is...

Thoughts and insights...

Tweaks to try next time...

Description: Story Starter is a recipe to jumpstart your imagination. You'll be using a visual cue to inspire a short story or tale.

Ingredients:
Journal
Photograph or picture from magazine or old greeting card with an image
A good writing pen
Kitchen timer

Directions:
1. Set your timer for 30–60 minutes.
2. Lay your pictures in front of you. Don't think, just pick up the one that jumps out at you.
3. Take a few minutes to look at the picture and listen—what story do you hear?
4. If that approach doesn't work for you, ask yourself what was going on in the scene the moment before this picture was taken.
5. Write the story.
6. When the timer goes off, you're done. Sign and date your page.

Hints & Options:
1. Don't worry, this recipe is not about grammar, it's about storytelling and finding your voice.
2. If you feel inspired to, use your spices to embellish your page.
3. Create a pocket in your journal where you can collect pictures and images that really inspire you, make you laugh, or speak to you on some level.
4. Great writers often wear vests or patched jackets...why not give it a try!

Recipe: Story Starter

What I like about this recipe is...

Thoughts and insights...

Tweaks to try next time...

Description: **Dab-It** is a fun recipe that takes the fear out of painting. All you do is "dab" your paint. Put a little paint on your brush and you create your whole picture by dabbing or tapping the brush on the paper. You may want to do this in two sessions.

Ingredients:
Journal (or thicker paper suggested)
Acrylic paints—kid paint is fine
3 paint brushes (try 3 different sizes with different shaped bristles)
Plastic plate or cardboard for paint tray
A picture from a magazine for inspiration
A cup of water
An old shirt so you don't get dirty
Kitchen timer

Directions:
1. Choose a time frame (30-90 minutes) and set your timer.
2. Place your magazine picture where you can see it.
3. Choose the color paint you want to use and put it on your plate/tray.
4. Start dabbing! Find your rhythm.
5. Remember to rinse your brush between colors.
6. Stand up and get some distance to see how your picture looks.
7. When your timer goes off, stop. Make sure to wash your brushes and find a safe place to let your picture dry.
8. Once dry, adhere your painting into your journal. Feel free to embellish however you like. Sign and date your page.

Hints & Options:
1. Do this recipe in two sessions. Use the second session for embellishing.
2. Put on music that inspires you and see how your Dabbing changes!

Recipe: Dab-It

What I like about this recipe is...

Thoughts and insights...

Tweaks to try next time...

Description: Mandala Speak recipe is an ancient form of self-expression. The word mandala comes from the Sanskrit word meaning "sacred circle." In **Mandala Speak** you will experience the power of your intuition.

Ingredients:
Journal, markers, colored pencils
A bowl that fits your journal page
Kitchen timer

Directions:
1. Choose your total time for this recipe (30–90 minutes).
2. Set your timer for 10 minutes less than your chosen time. Example: 30 minute session, set your timer for 20 minutes.
3. Find a spot in your journal to play and place your bowl upside down on your page and trace around it.
4. Cut your blank paper into 5 strips.
5. Write questions or statements on each of your 5 strips. For example: Question—Where do I start? Statement —When in darkness use your inner light.
6. Fold your questions and statements and place them in your bowl.
7. Now return to your circle. Take a deep breath and exhale. Begin to fill in the circle. You can pick a single shape, create a pattern, or draw a picture. There is no right or wrong.
8. When the timer goes off, stop what you're doing and reset the timer for 10 minutes.
9. Randomly pick a strip from your bowl and read it out loud.
10. Look at your Mandala. How does it answer your question or represent your statement? What insights do you have? Jot down your responses.
11. When your timer goes off, you're done. Sign and date your work.

Hints & Options:
1. If it feels overwhelming to draw within a big, blank circle, create sections within the circle. Focus on one section at a time.
2. Limit your color. Choose 1, 2, or 3 colors and stick with your choice.

Recipe: Mandala Speak

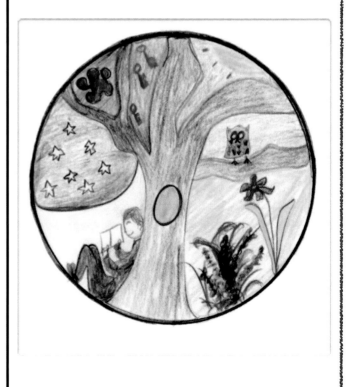

Venture Inwards

the rewards are great!

doodle, ponder, brainstorm...

thoma0m

Template: Dream Drop

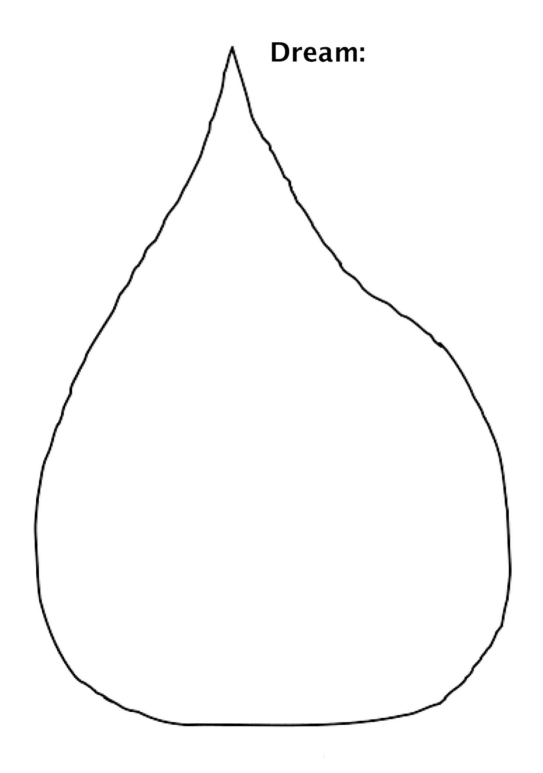

Dream:

Create a sacred space

make it visually inspiring

doodle, ponder, brainstorm...

Journal Maintenance

Now that you've learned the basics of Creative Journaling, here's a way to keep motivated, organized, and ready to enjoy a Creativity Snack whenever you have time. We all struggle with excuses and the most common ones I hear from clients are, "I don't have time" and "I don't know what to do," so I want you to think of this like you were trying to support healthy nutrition. It's much easier to enjoy your meals throughout the week if you plan ahead. Choose your recipes, shop, and prep so you're ready to go. Same goes for your Creative Snacking! Journal maintenance can be broken into weekly, monthly, or even quarterly efforts. Choose whatever best suits your schedule. As with everything else we've done, there is no right and wrong. See what works for you. Make your journal an inviting place to sit down and explore your thoughts and ideas while supporting yourself in Mastering the Art of Self-Expression.

Make a Recipe Card: Use an index card and list all the recipes you like. Place a number next to each one. When it's time for a snack, roll the dice. Whatever you roll is the snack you'll do. This eliminates the "I don't know what to do" excuse.

Rotate Your Ingredients and Spices: This will help you to keep your journal fresh. I like to set a budget for ingredients and spices. And sometimes I like to challenge myself to keep that budget really small. That way it becomes a game whenever I'm out shopping. I get to look through the sales bins and see if I can find something I like in my price range. Remember, some things are free. If you get a ticket stub or wrapper you like, put it in the spice bag. Change your spices at least quarterly to prevent them from becoming stale. Create a Snack Pack (check out my online class Creative Journaling 101 for tips on creating this fun storage idea).

Background Pages: Background pages can be done as a Creativity Snack. You can use anything you like. You could rubber or potato stamp a page. Paint a background or color one. The idea is to create a page that you could use as a background when doing another recipe.

Pictures: When you find pictures that really speak to you and you think you'd like to explore them through a Story Starter, just randomly glue them into your journal. Then when you're doing a snack just flip to a picture you like and get started.

Storage and Organization: For some people the randomness of Creative Journaling is challenging. If this is the case for you, you can create order in your journal a number of ways. Make tabs that divide your journal into sections so you can easily find the recipe you're looking for. Create pockets for images, quotes, or random bits of paper. You can create pockets from scratch, use envelopes, or buy the pre-made self-stick kind. Remember, there is no right or wrong way. Do what you find visually pleasing and inspiring and it will work out best for you!

Beauty begins the moment you decide to be yourself.
--Coco Chanel

doodle, ponder, brainstorm...

Glossary

Appetizer

A short recipe, a warm-up to get your creative juices flowing.

Background Page

A page you create visual texture on that will later be used as a foundation for a recipe.

Blind Challenge

Randomly choosing and using spices in a recipe.

Creative Journaling

A form of visual journaling that reconnects you to yourself by reclaiming your refrigerator art, exploring the power of play, and practicing consistent self-expression.

Creative Space

A sacred space that's just yours. Could be a room, a table, a TV tray, or a lap desk, etc.

Creativity Snack

A motivational, time management, and consistency tool.

Entrée

A longer recipe with more flavors and layers.

Ingredients

The general supplies you will collect for each recipe (markers, scissors, tape, colored paper, etc).

Recipe Page

A page that includes directions for a specific recipe as well as an ingredient list, samples, hints and options.

Refrigerator Art

The glorious results of creative self-expression, to be hung in a place of honor.

Snack

See Creativity Snack above.

Snack Pack

A container that holds ingredients and spices. Experiment with a variety of shapes and sizes for use at home or on the go (cigar box, file box, Tupperware container, lunch box).

Spices

The specialty flavors, random bits and pieces that add layer to a recipe (glitter, gems, stamps, ribbon, etc).

ThomaOm

A motivational mediative tool with pictures and words.

You create YOUR Road to Success!

If you enjoyed this workbook, check out my online class, *Creative Journaling 101*. In this class you'll learn about picking out your journal, snack packs, and more.

For more personal growth tools and online self-development classes visit laurathoma.com

Connect with me on social media:

Facebook: facebook.com/RoadtoSuccessWithLauraThoma

Twitter: twitter.com/LauraThoma

Instagram: instagram.com/roadtosuccess.live